THAI BOXING
DYNAMITE

THAI BOXING DYNAMITE

THE EXPLOSIVE ART OF MUAY THAI

ZORAN REBAC

That Boxing Dynamite
The Explosive Art of Muay Thai
by Zoran Rebac

Copyright © 1987 by Zoran Rebac

ISBN 0-87364-426-3
Printed in the United States of America

Published by Paladin Press, a division of
Paladin Enterprises, Inc., P.O. Box 1307,
Boulder, Colorado 80306, USA.
(303) 443-7250

Direct inquiries and/or orders to the above address.

First English Edition 1986
All Rights Reserved

Photographs by the author
Studio photographs by Dzenovic Davor
Drawings by the author
Translated by Brusar Kreshimir

First published by Paul H. Crompton Ltd., 638 Fulham Road,
  London SW6, England.
Tel.: 01 736-2551
Printed by Paladin Press by agreement with Paul H. Crompton, Ltd.

CONTENTS

6

FOREWORD

After thirteen years of practise and study of martial arts, I decided to extend my knowledge by practicing it in its fatherland, in Asia. For the last few years I have mainly been preoccupied with Thai boxing, so I went to Thailand and stayed there in February and March, 1983., practicing Muay Thai, as the Thais call their national sport. Throughout the world it is also known as Siamese Boxing, because Thailand was originally known as Siam.

At the Muang-Surin school of Thai Boxing I was accepted very cordially. During my stay I came across the idea of making a book and some of those photographs are included here. The rest of the photographs were made in Zagreb, Yugoslavia, after my return. I decided to write this book because in my country, as well as in Europe, there were no published books on this martial art, and I know there are many young martial artists who would like to know more about this unknown art.

The Muang-Surin school of Thai Boxing has the name of the province on the east of Thailand (near the Cambodia border), where it originated. It is one of the ten best known schools of Muay Thai in Thailand. At the moment this school has two national champions and several boxers on the top ten list. The majority of techniques practised in this school are presented in this book. Also, as technical differences between schools in Thailand and Kickboxing in Japan and USA are negligible, readers will be introduced to the basic methods of training which are almost the same anywhere. Therefore, those readers who will practice according to this book will be able to join any school of Thai Boxing or Kickboxing, provided that they master the techniques.

In writing this book I would like to thank my trainers Dentharonee Muangsurin, Chu Muangsurin, the promoter Sa Non, as well as all the boxers of Muang-Surin school, for their hospitality and regard during my stay in Thailand. I would also like to express gratitude to my friends who helped me realize this book: to Marijan Osman for technical arrangement, Davor Dzenovic for photographs, Toem Atachod, Savong Bundam and Zeljko Gvozdich for their help at demonstrating techniques.

Zagreb, 1983

Wall picture "scene from the court life" — prince Rangsit palace (17th century), shows Muay Thai match, accompanied by the music orchestra (right).

Muay Thai or Thai Boxing is a martial art over a 1000 years old. In combat it uses both hand and foot techniques. Old manuscripts describe eight basic tools of Thai Boxing: fists, elbows, knees and legs. Similar but less known martial arts are practiced in other Indochina countries; Laos, Cambodia, Burma (Bando Boxing), while Viet Vo Dao from Vietnam differs a lot, and is more similar to Karate. The history of Thai Boxing is connected with the migrations of the Thai tribe (meaning "free") in the 12th and 13th centuries from Juang-Xi, Sichuan and Hubei provinces in the south of China, into the present territory of Thailand. Migrations were particularly intensive in the thirteenth century under the pressures of Mongol hordes from the north. Therefore some sources assume that Thai Boxing has its origin in Chinese Boxing (Kung Fu), but that it has changed considerably. Other sources indicate that it originated during the period of incessant fights between the Thai Kingdom and their neighbouring Burma, Khmer and Cham (Vietnam) states. This hypothesis is quite likely as the need for martial art was greatest during that time.

An old Thai legend mentions a fighter named Nai Khon Don, who was captured by the Burmese and won freedom after winning barehanded against twelve Burmese gladiators. There is an annual tournament honouring him nowadays. According to the other legend from the 14th century, a fight between two boxers decided who would be the future king. It says that after the death of the old king Sen Muang Mu his sons Fang Keng and Ji Kumkam could not agree about the successor. As the conflict threatened to turn into civil war, the followers of each side agreed to stage a fight which would decide the future king. The fighter from the Ji Kumkam side won and Ji Kumkam thus became a king.

The oldest historical document mentioning Muay Thai as a warrior art comes from 1560 and describes a single combat between the Thai prince Naresuan (known as the Black Prince) and the successor to the Burmese throne, the son of the king Bayinnaung. The duel lasted several hours and ended with the death of the Burmese crown prince. Without the leader the Burmese decided not to attack Thailand. The reign of the king Pra-Chao Sua at the beginning of the 18th century, who was a very great master of the art himself, was a period of great development of Thai Boxing. It is said that the king, whose nick name was "Tiger", used to leave his palace secretly and attend local tournaments wearing a mask. He was a regular winner. In this period Thai Boxing was taught as a subject in all schools and was a part of military training. At that time fights were very cruel. There were no weight categories and rounds. Fighters were barefoot with their fists wrapped in hemp or cotton bandage. Genital protectors were made of coconut shells. All kinds of kicks and punches were allowed, with few limitations. Among other things, training included punching a lemon hitched on string for focus, kicking and punching palm trees in order to strenghthen feet and fists, long distance running, training in water, etc...

A special diet, mainly vegetarian was an obligation. Some techniques from that period remian unchanged until today and they are known as "king Tiger techniques". After World War II, Thai Boxing has changed a lot. Rule modifications transformed it into an attractive fighting sport, and many practice it as self defense or recreation.

Thais are very proud of their traditional martial art. Its popularity can be compared to that of basketball in Europe and the USA. Almost every male citizen knows at least the basics of this sport.

Thai Boxing differs from Karate and Kung Fu in several respects; Kicks and punches are delivered with full power and without holding back. Even today boxers fight barefoot, wearing only cotton anklets on their feet and boxing gloves on their hands. *Patterns, or so called "Katas", do not exist in Thai Boxing. Focus and power, timing and reflexes are developed by constant sparring practise, hitting the kicking and punching bags and pads, and participating in matches.* In order to avoid unnecessary injuries fighters wear protective equipment during sparring. Seeing how Thai Boxers practise, it is not difficult to understand why they usually win in matches with other styles. Music that is played during the matches and the traditional rituals before the fight give a special charm and distinction to Thai Boxing. The Orchestra that rhythmically follows the fight, consists of drums, cymbals and Jawa flutes. Of course every performer is well acquainted with Thai Boxing. Pre-fight ritual (wai kru) is performed according to the old habit. The boxer salutes the public with a gracious bow and flowing sweep of the hands to the head. After paying homage to his trainers, he performs a series of slow motion movements similar to dancing, which symbolize Muay Thai. "Wai kru" means "getting rid of fear from the heart" and the main purpose is to bring concentration to the fighters. The whole ritual lasts several minutes, and the school (camp) of the boxer can be recognized by his movements.

1

ph. 1 The beginning of the traditional ritual Wai kru

After the ritual, boxers go to the opposite sides of the ring where, instructed by their trainers and seconds, they wait for the sign of the gong. Immediately before starting they take off the "Mongkon", the cord that they wear around the head during the ritual, which is part of a traditional national garb. Another tradition is the habit of naming novice boxers according to their combativeness, temperament and character. A fighter's surname is the name of the school where he practises. Thus, for example, the present trainer of Muang-Surin school and the former champion of Thailand, fought under the name Dentharonee Sensak Muangsurin, which means "Dentharonee, winner of ten thousand fights, from Muang-Surin school". Nicknames, as is common in the Southeast Asia, have figurative meanings. Very common nicknames are tiger, green dragon, cobra, etc., and they symbolize some of the characteristics of a particular animal, like courage, speed or agility.

The fight lasts five rounds, each round lasts three minutes with two minute breaks. A referee controls the fight inside the ring, and there are two judges by the side. Points are summed at the end of each round, and the final sum decides the winner. If there is a knock down, which happens quite often, a referee counts to ten. Three knockdowns in one round mean the end of the match. There are matches on one of the two main stadiums in Bangkok, Rachadamneon or Lumpini, every day. Direct TV transmissions three times a week indicate the popularity of Thai Boxing. Many people watch the matches, and when top fighters fight, it is very difficult to obtain a ticket.

1A

ph.1a Boxer from the Luxilipat school, while performing Wai kru, wearing mongkon.

THAI BOXING AND OTHER MARTIAL ARTS

There are many martial arts in Asia, as almost every nation developed its own system of fighting. Therefore, it is important to indicate the position of Thai Boxing among a great number of eastern martial arts. Objective facts place it very high. I will describe the well known match between the selection of Kung Fu masters from Hong Kong and the team of Thai boxers, that took place in Bangkok, January 22, 1974. Fifteen thousand visitors at Hua Mark stadium saw only 6½ minutes of action in five fights. All five fighters from Hong Kong were knocked-out in the first round. Also a few months later a team from Singapore (Chang Tung style), some Japan and Philippines karatekas came to the same end. Singapore team included a fighter with the nickname "black killer", who, supposedly killed an opponent in an unofficial tournament. But he was also knocked out in the first round. There was a match in Manilla, Philippines, between karate champion Kandido Picate and Thai boxer Nirund Bunjanet. Karate champion of the Philippines fell down to the floor twice in the first round, and was knocked out in the second. Match was televised.

Similar fights between different styles took place several decades ago. There are written documents about the fight in 1921 between Chinese Master Tse Shang from Guandong province who had a reputation of high control of "chi", and Thai boxer Ian Hantaley. The Chinese Master lost the match and had to undergo several months of medical care to recover. In 1959, a team of Tai Kek style fighters from Formosa lost the match with Thai team with the first round k.o. again. *One may wonder about the reasons for such successes. The answer does not lie in the superiority of techniques by themselves. It is in the way they are practised.*

In Thai Boxing everything is practised with a realism that is lacking in all non-contact sports. Thai boxers in sparring and in matches deliver and receive many kicks and punches. The knowledge of the art must be proved in the ring. It is obvious that knowledge and experience attained in this way cannot be compensated for by any other method. Some readers may ask whether Thai Boxing is a very good method of self defence.

An episode that was published in almost every Bangkok newspaper can serve as a good answer. Coming home, a young man was surrounded by a group of robbers that have for quite a long time terrorised one of the suburbs in Bangkok. He defended himself barehanded, and two attackers ended up in hospital with broken ribs, a third with a broken jaw, others ran away, but were soon caught by the police. The courageous young man was a Muay Thai boxer and he ended with only a torn shirt and several bruises. But this type of story should not be taken for granted. Those who practice Thai Boxing are not "supermen".

Still, with full determination, concentration and some luck, much can be done in difficult situations. Nowadays Thai Boxing is becoming a fighting sport, more than an art.

"Chi" — in Chinese language internal power.

2

ph. 2 First page of one of a popular Muay Thai magazine.

3

ph.3 Right: Dentharonee Muangsurin, one of the best known
Muay Thai trainers in Bangkok

First I would like to emphasize that Thai Boxing terminology is not worked out in detail as in some other martial arts. Instead of full names, Thais usually use abbreviations that denote a particular technique. They also use descriptive names which is usual in many Asian countries. Thus, all kinds of round kicks they call "crocodile tail's kick". I decided to use abreviations and short names because the Thai language is very complicated and the reader would not have much need of learning the names of techniques in Thai. They can be very well described in other languages, too. Therefore, I think that the book will be more understandable if I write for example; make a punch and two knee kicks, instead of Thai terms "chok, son kao".

While learning basic techniques, it is important to follow a certain order. Every block, punch or kick should be first learned technically, i.e. slow and correct in the beginning, while speed and power are gradually added through practice. To achieve maximum effect, it is necessary to coordinate loosening and contraction of muscles with inhaling and exhaling. It should also be kept in mind that almost all kinds of kicks and punches are performed with rotation of body and hips. With such practice, power of leg or arm is increased with the mass of the whole body. Without application of these principles it is not possible to achieve maximum speed and power.

Unlike the majority of martial arts, Thai Boxing has only one stance. It is used in fighting and all the techniques could be performed from it. The stance has a shoulder width and length about half a metre, depending on the height of the fighter. Body weight is equal on both feet. The body is kept upright and slightly sideways while hands are kept in front of the head. Elbows must be tight to the body as much as it is possible, and the head is slightly bent forward. This stance ensures maximum protection of head and body. While fighting, it is necessary to move constantly as it is much more difficult to hit a moving target than a stationary one. Moving on tiptoes the fighter should be able to dodge and attack at any moment. It is recommended not to cross the feet during fighting as this position makes the fighter unstable and prevents easy movements. If the fighter is right handed, he should choose the stance with his left foot in front (left lead posture), while for southpaw boxers the stance with the right foot in front (right lead posture) is chosen.

Hands should never be dropped down as the fighter risks being hit on the unprotected head or body. Essentially, this stance is natural and does not require much learning. It enables maximum mobility and efficiency.

Drawings A, B, C, D show methods of moving forward, backward and sideways. Starting stance is with the right foot in front. While moving forward, front foot steps first, when moving backwards back foot steps first. When moving sideways to the left, left foot steps first, and right foot steps first when moving to the right.

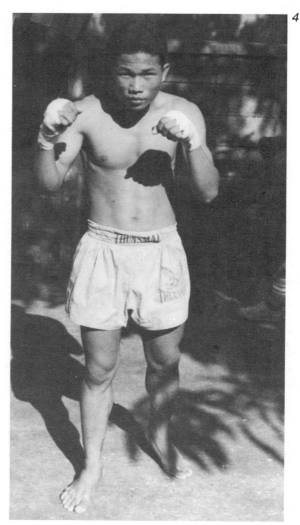

4

ph.4 This is the fighting stance of Thai boxers. The right leg is in front (right lead posture), which is usually for southpaw boxers.

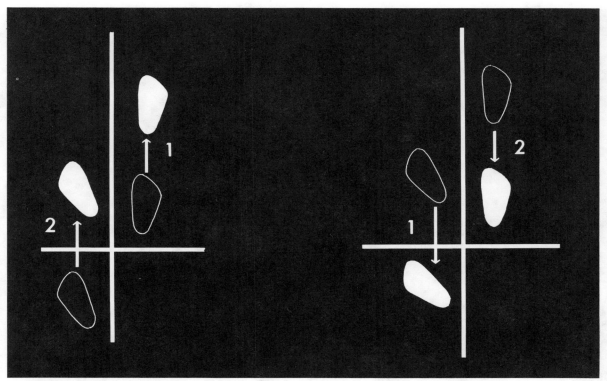

drawing A — Advance shuffle
Front foot steps forward about half a step, and then back foot is moved. The sequence of such small steps makes forward movement while always keeping fighting stance.

drawing B — Backward shuffle
Back foot steps back first, (from the basic posture) and then front foot follows. This is moving backwards in order to assume a better position, or to retreat.

By moving sideways we can evade an opponent's attacks and circle around him.

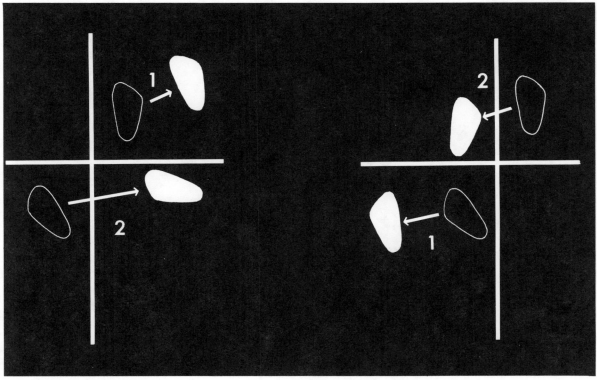

drawing C — Moving to the right
Front foot is moved to the right and a little to the front, and then the left foot is moved.

drawing D — Moving to the left
Back foot is moved to the left and a little to the back, and then front foot is moved.

ph.5. Powerful straight punch produced the opponent's knockdown.

Straight punch (chok)

It is one of the most used punching techniques in Thai Boxing. This punch can be used for several purposes: for checking (stopping) the attack, for making a chance for an attack, for disturbing the opponent and also as the final punch which can cause knock-out. It can be delivered from the stance with the front fist (straight punch or jab) or with back fist (reverse straight punch) photos 6,7. It is usually performed in series of at least three punches. In the beginning it is important to be relaxed, and then to deliver the punch by quickly rotating the body. At the same time care should be taken that the other hand guards the head, being positioned in front of the head.

After the attack, the hand is withdrawn in the shortest possible way. It is important that punches are always executed in series and not as singles. A series is continued until the opponent is knocked out or starts to counterattack. After learning to punch without a target, practice should be continued on punching bag and pads.

A well trained boxer can answer the opponent's attack with two or three of his own. The main aim is the opponent's head, not body, as bending forward in order to punch into the body increases the risk of being hit by a knee or grabbed. Sometimes straight punches are executed simultaneously with foot techniques (photo 8.) or in a combination.

6

7

Hook punch and uppercut (mat tong, mat aat)

These punches are based on the same principles as straight punch. They should also be learned in the same way.

In matches they are not seen as often as straight punches, as they require close distance which increases the risk of being hit or grabbed. Following photos show hook punch (ph.9) and uppercut (ph.10). Main target is again opponent's head. Uppercut is primarily a surprise punch. Series of photos (11-15) show how these punches are practiced on the punching bag. After two fast straight punches (right and left) the third in a series can be hook or uppercut.

9

10

11

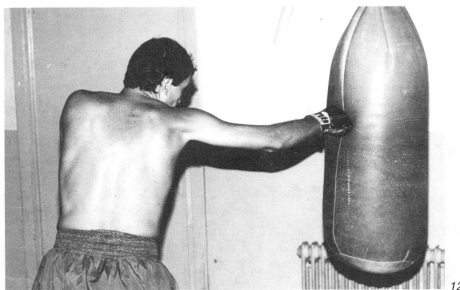

12

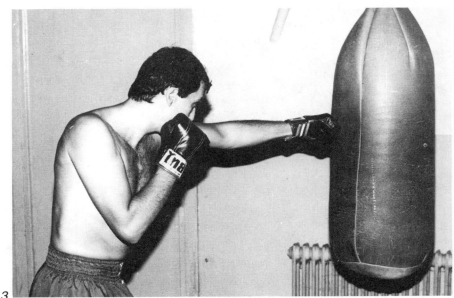

13

14

15

Below: In close distance fighting, boxers take very much care about head protection. Fighter on the left found a gap and delivered an uppercut.

Elbow strike (sok)

Elbow strike is one of the most powerful and dangerous weapons in close fighting. In Thai Boxing there are three basic elbow strikes: side strike (ph.17), downward strike (ph.18) and upward strike (ph.19). Sometimes a jumping elbow strike can be seen, or the turning elbow strike, but these techniques belong to special advanced techniques and this book is not focused on them.

Elbow strikes are performed following the same principles as with other hand techniques. Power is generated by the rotation of the whole body. Strikes can be executed with the front or back elbow (from the basic stance), depending on the fighting situation. Photo 16 shows side elbow strike (with front elbow) in a real match. It is best to practice elbow strikes on the punching bag. As they are never used as the starting punch in attack (they are relatively short ranged), they should be practiced as the second or third punch in a series, for example after a straight punch. They can also be practiced as a counter-attack. Its primary target is the opponent's head and then other parts of the body. Photos 20, 21 show how this strike is practiced on a punching bag. From a basic stance we strike with the right elbow (back elbow).

Through rotation we apply the whole mass of the body (techniques are demonstrated by the boxer from Cambodia where there is a similar art to Thai Boxing which is called Muay Khmer). Elbow strikes should be practiced so that the right elbow strike immediately follows the left elbow strike and vice versa. Photos 22, 23, 24 show preparation and two fast successive elbow strikes (first with right and then with left elbow). Strikes are performed by stepping forward slightly.

16

17

20

21

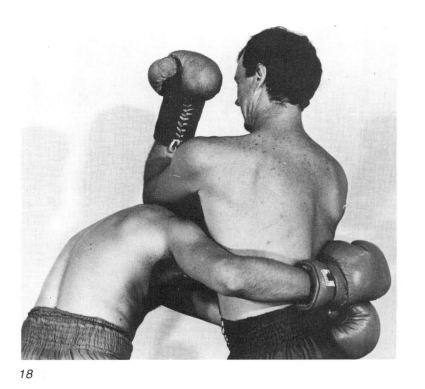

18

19

22

23

24

There are several basic rules that should be taken into account while performing foot techniques. The way the kicks are delivered in Thai Boxing is slightly different from other martial arts. Thai Boxing kicks are the so called piercing kicks. They are executed as if cutting (chopping) the opponent, and also there is no stopping while practicing with an imaginary opponent (shadow boxing) or as the Thais say dtoi-lom (boxing with the wind). Unlike Karate or Kung Fu, there are no snap kicks in Muay Thai. Round kick, the most popular kick in Thai Boxing, characterises the Thai way of kicking. While kicking, great attention is paid to head protection, as every counter attack is dangerous if we stay on one foot only. Therefore, Thai boxers always kick with protected head and body. Also, you must keep in mind that all foot techniques should be performed standing on the tiptoes of the supporting leg, which enables greater speed. In many books on martial arts you can find a recommendation that the foot of the supporting leg should not be raised on tiptoes during kicking, in order to have better balance and power. This advice is not quite good, as balance (during the short period of delivering the kick) can be retained on tiptoes too. In fact power depends on energy that we can generate and the short period of time during which the energy is transmitted to the target. (In reality, it depends on the speed of the kick). Physical law expresses it as formula: $P = E/t$ or $P = m \cdot a \cdot v$.

P — power, E — energy, t — time, m — mass, a — acceleration, v — speed.

It can be concluded that, in order to deliver a powerful punch or kick, man need not be particularly strong. A kick executed by a person two times faster will be as powerful as that of a man two times stronger but twice as slow. And isn't it common that smaller people are faster than bigger? If the kick is slow, it turns into pushing, and only then should the whole foot be on the ground. *In practice, power and speed of the kick are generated by a good start at the first phase, and putting the whole mass of the body into the kick, by rotation of hips and contracting the muscles at the end. To start well, it is necessary to bounce powerfully from the floor with the kicking foot. This makes the starting acceleration, while the rotation of hips accelerates the kick further to achieve maximum speed while contacting the target.*

24A

Front kick (tiip)

The application of this kick among kicking techniques is the same as that of straight punch among punching techniques. It can be used as the finishing kick, as the kick for provoking the opponent, or creating openings, for stopping the attack, and in a series of hand and foot techniques. Ball of the foot, heel, and in some cases the whole foot are used as tools in this kick. Photos 26, 27, 28 show how it is performed. After bouncing (springing) from the floor, the kicking foot goes in at the height of the supporting leg's knee. The body is rotated slightly to the side, which lengthens the range of the kick. Arms protect head and body. From the basic stance a front kick can be executed with the front or back foot (ph. 29).

The kick with the front foot usually stops the opponent's attack, while the back foot is used to deliver a more powerful kick, when it is obvious that the opponent cannot dodge. If we want to attack with the combination of kicks, then the front kick is good as a starting kick. Primary targets are the solar plexus and abdomen (ph. 30), and sometimes the chin, though it is dangerous to try to attack an experienced opponent in this way. Jumping front kick is the variation of the front kick, but it is used very rarely and is an advanced technique. Photo 25, a scene from the match: the boxer on the left side has delivered a successful front kick thus throwing off the opponent who has tried to attack with the round kick.

25

26

27

28

29

After mastering the techniques of performing this kick without the target, it is best to practise it on the kicking bag in combination with other kicks (ph. 32).

While practicing without a target, it is not recommendable to kick with full power as knee joints can be injured. Photo 33 shows how this kick is practised on kicking pads.

30

32

31

33

No martial art in Asia has so widely developed knee kicks as Thai Boxing. It is a most powerful weapon at close range and boxers use it whenever they have an opportunity. Rarely can someone endure the devastating series of these kicks once he is grabbed by the opponent. There are several kinds of knee. The broadest distinction is between kicks with grabbing the opponent, and those without grabbing. According to the way they are performed there are: front knee kicks, round knee kicks and jumping knee kicks. All these kicks can be seen very often in matches. Primary targets are head and body, also part of the leg above the knee. Great attention and a big part of training programmes are devoted to the practice of knee techniques. Photos 34, and 35 show how to grab an opponent while delivering a knee kick.

Corectly grabbed, the opponent is in a very dangerous position and it is very hard to release. First, the opponent is grabbed by the neck with hands crossed on his back (ph.34). Then we lean against him with our forearms on his chest, bending his head down, and simultaneously jerk him down and kick him with the knee (ph.35). The opponent can be attacked in the head with the knee kick (ph.38), the body (ph.39) and round knee kick into the body (ph.40)

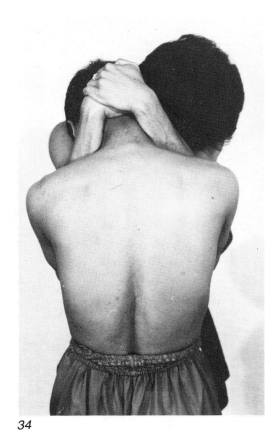

34

35

Grabbing is called "djab ko". Though seemingly simple, this technique requires very much practice.

36

ph. 36: A scene from the match — jumping knee kick blocked at the very last moment.

38

39

40

37

After the opponent is grabbed, it is possible to attack him in several ways. Every way can cause a knock out ("fet rao"). Targets are opponent's head, solar pelxus and ribs.

41   42

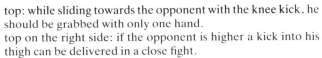

top: while sliding towards the opponent with the knee kick, he should be grabbed with only one hand.

top on the right side: if the opponent is higher a kick into his thigh can be delivered in a close fight.

43

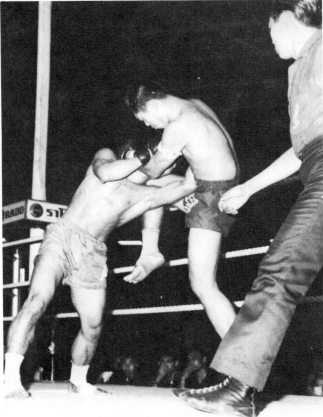

ph. 43 — a scene from the match: successfully delivered knee kick into the opponent's head. Many matches end with such a knock out.

44

45

While kicking into the head it is important to bend the opponent down enough so that we can reach his head with our knee. Therefore, he should be powerfully and suddenly pulled downward and forward. A variant of front knee kick is the kick while sliding toward the opponent and grabbing him with only one hand (ph.41). It is used when the opponent bends forward by himself, or it he is forced to bend after a series of attacks. It is important to choose the right moment to attack and great fighting experience is necessary. Another variant is a knee kick while grabbing the opponent around the waist. It is mainly used for attacking the thigh (ph.42). Photo 43 shows a successfully delivered knee kick with grabbing. Knee kick without grabbing is also a very popular technique in Thai Boxing. It can be used as the finishing kick in the attack, or as counter attack. Ph. 44, 45 show how this technique is performed, and photo 46 shows the usage of this kick as a counter. Again, it is important that hands protect the head and that the instep of the kicking leg as well as the supporting leg are stretched.

Front knee kick without grabbing is successful in both the attack and defense. Photo on the left shows how it can be used as the defense from the straight punch.

46

Photograph at the bottom of the page: a scene from the match. The boxer on the left side is stopped with a powerful knee kick into the body.

47

48

49

50

While practicing knee kick, arms should be pulled power-fully downward and to the side. Photographs on the right show two basic knee kicks with grabbing, while performed without the partner. Front knee kick (ph.49) and side knee kick (ph.51) are based on the same principle and are usually combined.

51

52

53

While kicking, body weight is on tiptoes of the supporting leg. Rotation and springing start principles are used in knee kicks too. A Knee kick without grabbing has a little bit longer range because we stretch forward while kicking. Photos from matches show successfully delivered attack (ph.33), and counter with knee kick before the boxer on the left side succeeded to attack with the hook punch (ph.47). Jumping knee kicks are among the greatest skills. They can be made by jumping directly, or with the step. It is performed so that one foot springs as much as possible from the ground, while the other delivers a kick into the opponent's head or body. Photograph 48 shows a very attractive moment in a fight, that needs no comment. All these kicks should first be practiced without the target and then they should be perfected on kicking pads and bags. Photo 49 shows a boy practicing front knee kick with imaginary grab. (Thais start learning Muay Thai when they are very young). Knee techniques should be practiced in series of five or six kicks, and also in combinations with other kicks.

Practice on a hard kicking bag can be very painful and exhausting in the beginning. However everybody must know that nothing can be achieved without hard work. After a few months of regular training, knees will harden and transform into real weapons. Many boxers in Thailand have knees hardened to the point that is unbelievable to us Europeans. Photograph 52 shows a knee kick without grab, this time into a kicking bag. (All the elements that we pointed out can be seen here: arms protecting head, instep of the kicking leg is stretched, body weight is on tiptoes of supporting foot.)

Photograph 53 shows a front knee kick with a grab. The kicking bag is grabbed at the height of the opponent's head. Elbows are kept close together, head close to the bag (in reality near the opponent's head so that we can avoid eventual punches or elbow strikes). Springing fast we kick the bag in series. It is necessary to practise with all the movements that are used in a real fight. The kicking bag may be pushed, pulled, circled etc.... The way Thai Boxers kick the bag is very imaginative and it is difficult to describe it with photographs. This can only be learned by visiting a Muay Thai camp.

54

Round kick (te)

It is the most widely used technique in Thai Boxing. It is said that this technique symbolized Thai Boxing. Veteran boxers call it the king of all kicks. The tool is the whole shin and instep. Shin is used for kicking into the body, while instep is for kicks into the head and neck. Photos 55, 56, 57, show how to perform this kick. The kicking foot starts suddenly from the fighting stance, with simultaneous rotation of the hips and body. The supporting leg must be completely stretched at the moment of impact, while body weight is on the tiptoes and ball of the foot. Head and body are protected by the arms. Full turn is made when this kick is practiced in the manner of shadow boxing, while the foot is returned the same way when practicing on the kicking bag. Round kick in Thai Boxing differs from those in other kicking martial arts (for example Karate or Taekwon-Do).

They are executed with the swing of the whole body, and not only with the snap of the lower leg below knee. The power of such a kick is sometimes so strong that it cannot be stopped even with a double arm block. It is the most powerful kick in Thai Boxing and can be used for an attack on any part of the body. Photographs 58 and 59 show round kick to the inner and outer part of the thigh, both inevitable techniques of Thai boxers.

55

56

57

58

60

59

Most common targets are the opponent's head, neck, body or legs. Round kick into the opponent's thigh is called "djog yan", meaning "piercing a pair of bellows".

61 Ph. 60, 61 show round kicks into the body and head. It is particularly important to protect head and body against a counter.

62

A scene from the match: Jumping round kick is delivered to the opponent's body. This kind of kick is called "kradot te". Great power is generated fromt the jump towards the opponent. Such a kick is best used when the opponent is unbalanced or when he is retreating. It can be also used as a surprise kick. Boxers who can use this kick in a real fight are very respected. Many Japanese Kickboxers consider low round kick a very important tactical weapon. After several rounds of receiving powerful low kicks, a boxer unaccustomed to this kind of fighting cannot even stand on his feet, nor can he deliver any kicks. This tactic is very well illustrated by the old Thai Boxing proverb: "The opponent who cannot stand, cannot fight".

A special kind of round kick is a jumping kick (ph.62). One foot springs in the air while the kick is executed with another.

It is important to resume a stable position after delivering jumping kick, so that we can be able to continue the attack or react to the opponent's counterattack. After perfecting this kick by practicing without target, it is a must to continue on kicking and punching bag and pads, (ph. 63, 64, 65). Thai Boxers usually spend hours practicing different combinations of this kick. A series of a few kicks with the same leg is very popular. This kick also requires several months of hard practice as it is necessary to strengthen shins for kicking or blocking. Experienced boxers can permanently attack the opponent, however hard his blocks are. Following photographs are scenes from the matches: (ph.66) — successfully delivered round kick into the opponent's thigh. It seems that the power of the kick raised the opponent from the floor (ph.67).

64

63

65

66

67

Side kick (tiip)

It is interesting that the Thais use the same name for this technique as for the front thrusting kick, although there is a great difference in the way they are performed. But from the point of view of practical application, these differences disappear. The side kick can be useful in the same fighting situations as the front kick, and the only difference is in kicking tools. The primary tool for the side kick is footsword (edge of the foot) and heel. Still, it must be emphasized that Thai boxers use this kick very rarely. Even though I attended more than two hundred matches, I saw this technique only a few times, mainly as a counter attack. Some of the Thai boxers can deliver spin kicks, too, but never try that against the opponent in the ring. Photo 68 is a rarity. It was taken in Lampoon, in Northern Thailand, a few miles from the border of Laos. Most of the Thai boxing camps did not incorporate this kick in their training program. My trainers,

Dentharonee Muangsurin and Surapong Harmnyom (trainer of the Singprasout camp—"School of Grand Lion"—in Chiang Mai where I was in 1985) told me that the opinion of the majority of Muay Thai teachers is that this kind of kick is too risky. They explain their attitude in the following way: "While performing this technique, the boxer's body faces the opponent sideways, and in case his attack has been blocked or missed, the boxer is not able to continue with punching techniques. Cooperation between hands and feet in Muay Thai is of the most importance!"

Students of many other styles became convinced that this comment is true by testing it themselves. Keeping this in mind, it is not strange why Thai boxers do not care much about the side kick, while on the contrary, in karate and taekwondo it is one of the basic techniques!

68

This chapter is about Thai Boxing defence techniques against different attacks. Part of every training is devoted to these techniques, *as it is not enough to know how to deliver strikes, but also to avoid or block them and to counter attack.* It is most important to stay calm while awaiting the opponent's attack, otherwise we would not be able to react correctly. The whole body of the opponent should be encompassed by our vision. One of the mistakes that many people make while being attacked is blinking. Thus they lose time for right reaction, and the opponent usually hits the target. This mistake can be avoided by consciously trying not to blink during training. Some schools, especially in the south of Thailand, continue the traditional method of training the fighters not to blink.

Boxers enter the sea, up to their waist, and bending over the surface with their eyes open, clap their palms and try not to blink. This exercise gives excellent results.

Another thing that is very important for good defence is intuition, or ability to anticipate the moment of the opponent's attack. The very mechanism of intuition is not yet quite elucidated. Many martial arts legends mention the sixth sense, that can be developed through certain exercise. Some trainers misuse this, and lure the students by some special mystical exercises, while neglecting practice in reality. There are no proofs yet about the sixth sense but it is known that animals in some cases can anticipate danger. One thing is certain though, intuition, more or less powerful, can only be attained through years of hard training. Many boxers who have several years of fighting experience can feel the moment of the opponent's attack and can prevent it with their own. This is a higher level of defence than blocking and counterattacking. Therefore, after mastering various defence techniques, we must make efforts in that way.

A powerful elbow counter attack is the answer to the opponent's attack in both examples. The defense in the second example is harder to master, but is more efficient. Elbow strikes are ideal self defence weapons.

3

1

4

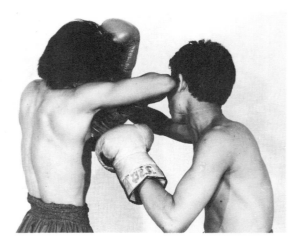

2

5

As it is necessary to come close to the opponent in order to attack with the straight punch, all kinds of strikes of short or long range are useful defence weapons. The next four examples show defence against straight punch, using short range weapons (elbow and knee). The following two examples show the defence against straight punch by using long range weapons (front and round kick) as counter attacks. Each defence has its advantages depending on the fighting situation; for example the distance between fighters, room for delivering kicks and punches, etc. Photos 1 and 2 show simple but very efficient defences against straight punches. In ph.1 a straight punch is blocked with the left hand, and an elbow strike counter attack is show in ph.2. Photos 3, 4 and 5 show similar defences, this time without blocking. Opponent's punch is avoided by semi-circular downward and sideways bending (ducking). While the punch misses the head, we are in a good position to deliver a side elbow strike. It is important that ducking and elbow strike counter attacks should be performed continually.

A very useful close distance counter attack against a straight punch is a knee kick. Photos 6, 7, 8 show defences by using knee counterattacks. Photos 6 and 7 show how to move forward blocking the straight punch with outer forearm block (moving the forearm inside out). At the same time a knee kick is delivered into the opponent's body.

6

7

8

Defence in photo 8 is based on the same principle, but this time the straight punch is blocked with the inner forearm block (movement of the forearm from the outside in). Straight punches can be successfully stopped with long range kicks. This kind of defence is safer, as kicks can be delivered from the greater distance, out of the range of a straight punch. It is very important to react at the right moment, because late reaction enables the opponent to startle the defender when he has one foot in the air. Phtos 9 and 10 show how to stop a straight punch with a round kick. The opponent's right punch is stopped with the right palm and at the same time a round kick counter attack is executed into the opponent's body. Left arm should be stretched so that the opponent can be kept at a safe distance. Front kick can also stop a straight punch (photo 11). At the moment when the opponent prepares for the attack, front kick should be executed. It is best to kick into solar plexus or abdomen. Arms should be kept protecting head and body, as the opponent may not be stopped with only one kick. Some boxers can endure very powerful kicks, but a series of well delivered kicks will force even strong opponents to start to defend themselves, or to attack more cautiously.

9

10

11

Ph.11: While stopping the opponent's attack with the front kick it must be kept in mind that the kick should be delivered at the right time. The kick executed too early or too late is more dangerous for the executer than for his opponent. As soon as the kick hits the target, it should be withdrawn, to avoid the opponent's seizure of the foot. When kicking with the ball of the foot, toes should be bent back to avoid injuries.

In close distance, an elbow strike is one of the most dangerous weapons, and responsible for the greatest number of injuries in matches. Therefore, Thai Boxers pay great attention to defence against elbow strikes. The easiest way to avoid elbow strikes is to move backwards and then attack from a safer distance with one of the foot techniques. But there are also some effective defences when there is not enough space for withdrawal. In the first example an elbow strike is stopped with the double forearm block (photo 12) and immediately after, a knee kick is delivered into the opponent's ribs, (photo 13).

12

13

Photos 14-17 show how an elbow strike is blocked with the right hand and how to counter attack with the hook punch, or left elbow strike.

14

15

Danger of elbow strike attacks is also one of the reasons why arms should always be kept in front of the head. After blocking, not lowering the arms, a counter attack is performed with hook or side elbow strike (sok trong). If the opponent evades this attack he can still be hit with the back elbow strike. Other elbow strikes (upward and downward) Thais call "sok kun" and "sok lon".

16

17

Front kick defence is mainly based on blocking, grabbing the opponent's leg and dodging. Photos 18-20 show how to block front kick with downward block (downward and sideways movement of the hand). While blocking, it is important not only to stop the opponent's kick, but also to put him into a state of unbalance by wiping his leg aside.

After blocking, a low round kick should be delivered into his thigh. The right time to counter attack is the moment when the opponent is unbalanced. Following example (photos 21, 22) shows grabbing of the front kick and knee kick counter. After sidestepping (see drawing C in "Stance and movements" chapter) leg is powerfully grabbed and kept close to the body so that the opponent cannot release himself. While holding the opponent's neck with the right hand he should be powerfully jerked downwards and kicked with the knee (ph.22).

18

19

20

Close fighting with knee kicks is a speciality of Thai Boxing. There is no match where one does not see boxers holding each other and exchanging a series of knee kicks. Sometimes fighters spend the whole round fighting with knees, only. Those who have not tried themselves do not know how exhausting this kind of fight is. There are many defenses against knee kicks; blocks, releases from grabbing, evading, and different kinds of throwing. Pushing and dragging the opponent in order to assume better position or to unbalance him is of very great importance. Very common tactics is clinching and not allowing the opponent to attain space needed for kicking. Photos 23 and 24, show inner shin block (moving the shin inside) and outer shin block (moving the shin out), which are two main blocks against a knee kick. In some situations knee kicks can be blocked with elbows and forearms, but as they are very powerful, it is hard to stop them (photo 25). Photograph 26 shows shin block in a real fight.

23

24

25

Stopping the knee kick; forearm block (up), shin block
(down).
Shin block is called "buok" or "kaak"

26

Series of photos 27-31 show release from grabbing. This very important technique is based on putting the hand through the opponent's "embrace" and then releasing by jerking outside with the elbows.

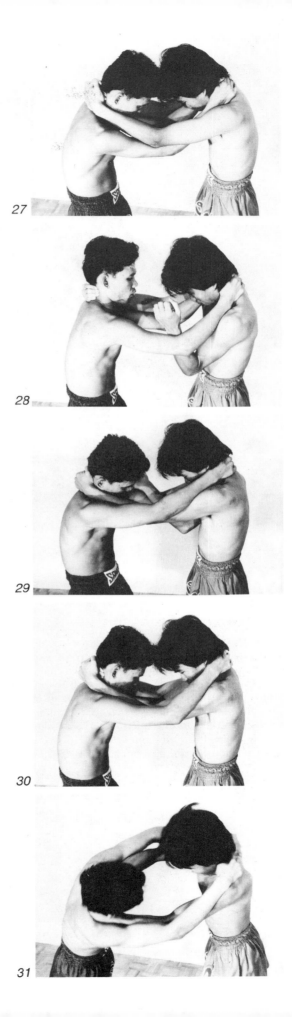

27

28

29

30

31

Photos 27: The opponent grabs you by the neck. Hands should be put inside the opponent's grab, one by one, (photos 28, 29). Care should be taken about a possible knee kick. Now, you are in an advantageous position to release yourself from the grab, and to unbalance the opponent (photo 31). If the first release does not succeed, another should be tried immediately, but this time jerking to the other side. By pushing the opponent away you can release yourself, before you are too strongly grabbed and kicked (photo 32).

32

Front knee kicks without grabbing are usually avoided by retreating or dodging to the side (photo 33), and then a counter attack can be made, mostly with hand techniques. Photo 34 shows a similar defence, this time with forearm block and straight punch counter to the opponent's body or head. Different throwing techniques are special kinds of defence against knee kick. The first example (photo 35-40) shows how knee kick is stopped with forearm or elbow (ph.37) and how, immediately afterwards, the opponent is grabbed with the same arm and held around the neck with the other (ph.38). After sidestepping we can throw him with a powerful semicircular jerk (photo 39, 40). In the following example knee kick is avoided by rotating the body to the right (photo 43). Using the advantageous position when the opponent's foot is still in the air, we should unbalance him by powerfully jerking and throwing him down. It is very important to hold him strongly by the neck in the beginning, (photo 41-46).

33

34

35

36

37

Throwing techniques, called "thum", are in the repertoire
of Thai boxers, and can be seen in almost every match. The
technique shown in these photographs is one of the most frequent. Sidestepping move and jerk are performed as one
movement.

The same technique from the previous page, but this time from a real fight. The leg of the boxer on the left side is powerfully grabbed and he is going to fall down soon.

Photos at the bottom of the page: Six phases of throwing by avoiding the knee kick. Crucial moments are evasion (ph.43) and starting phase of throwing (ph.44).

41

42

43

46

45

44

47

48

49

In previous chapters the round kick was already decribed as the most frequently used technique in Thai Boxing, therefore, it is not unusual that there are many ways of defence against round kick attacks. Round kick can be blocked in several ways. It is very often blocked with the shin part of the leg. Two kinds of shin block are shown on photographs 47 and 48. Photo 47 show how round kick is blocked by moving the shin out, and photo 48, how it is blocked by moving the shin in. Both ways are equally efficient and their usage depends on the fighting situation. In order to be able to block with shins, it is necessary to harden them by practicing on the kicking bags. During blocking the arms are protecting the head, and together with the shin make an obstacle for the round kick. High section round kicks are usually blocked with the fore-arms (photo 50), or are avoided by retreating and dodging to the side. The best defence is preventing the kick with our own kick or punch.

Photo 49, a scene from a match. Round kick is blocked with the shin.

50

51

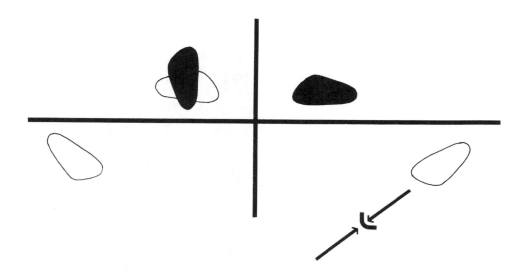

Photos 51 and 52 show outer shin block against round kick attack. The opponent attacks with the right round kick. The defender blocks by moving his left shin out (ph. 51 and draw-ing A), and then with a small step forward and to the side, delivers a counter kick with the other leg, (ph. 52 and drawing B).

52

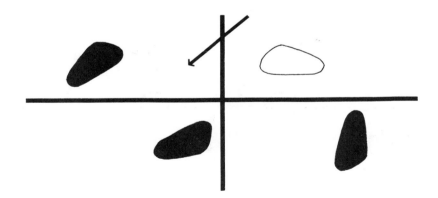

53

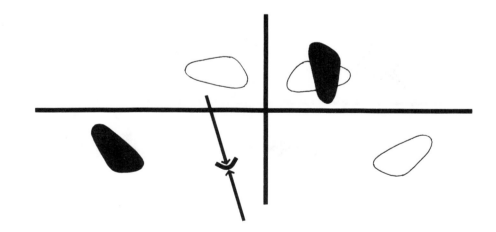

54

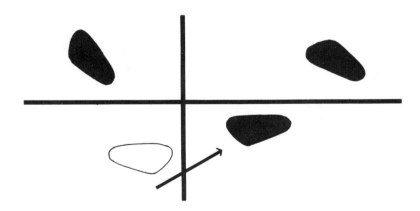

Photos 53 and 54 show a similar defence, this time with inner shin block against round kick attack. The opponent attacks with the left round kick. By quickly moving his shin inside, the defender stops the kick. Immediately dropping the blocking leg, he steps to the side and forward, and delivers a counter kick with the right foot, (Ph. 54 and drawing D).

55

Photo 55 shows a relatively simple defence technique, with the forearm block and straight punch counter into the opponent's head or body. It is important to step in, at the right moment, and block the round kick before it gains full power. Stepping forward makes a closer distance from which it is possible to deliver a straight punch. In a real fight it is necessary to contiue with a series of kicks and punches after defending. Round kick can be successfully avoided by simple retreating, (photo 56). Immediately after the opponent's kick misses, a counter attack should be delivered into his head or body, (photo 57). It is important not to retreat too much, as the distance would be too great for a successful counter attack. And now one of the specialities of Thai Boxing (photo 58, 59). Only the most experienced boxers can use this technique in matches. As the opponent attacks with the round kick into the head, the defender steps to the left side with his left foot and kicks the attacker's leg with his shin or instep. It is very important to be faster than the opponent and to feel the moment of his attack. Correctly executed a kick should throw the attacker down.

56

57

58

59

60

61

Trainer Dentharonee Muangsurin demonstrates a similar technique, but this time blocking with his forearms, which is safer for the defender. After blocking the kick (photo 60) he counter attacks with a low kick to the upper part of the attacker's leg, when his foot is still in the air. Photo 62: a scene from a match. Perfectly executed counter attack on the opponent's leg. In photographs 63-66 the author of this book demonstrates another defence against a round kick attack. He blocks the kick first, then counter attacks by kicking the opponent's thigh, this time on the outer side. Again, arms protect head and body.

62

63

64

65

66

67

68

In the ring boxers who successfully grab the opponent's leg very often powerfully push the opponent to the ropes, and then start series of kicks with knees.

69

70

When the opponent's kicks are slow there is a chance to grab him and put him into a very bad situation. Photos 67 and 68 show how the opponent is counter attacked with the left knee while the defender holds his leg. Immediately after contact, the kicking knee should be withdrawn so that another kick can be delivered. Quick withdrawal also prevents the foot from being grabbed. In photo 69 the attacker's kick is blocked and his foot grabbed immediately afterward. Kicking his leg with the shin is the counter-attack, (photo 70).

Photo 71, a scene from a match: the fighter on the right side grabbed the opponent's leg and a counter attack follows.

71

Round kick can be stopped with the simultaneous front kick counter (photo 72, 73) or photo 25 in the chapter "Front kick — (tiip)". At the moment when the attacker's kicking foot is in the middle of the path, we slide toward him and deliver front kick. Correctly executed techniques will certainly unbalance the opponent and if he is kicked powerfully enough, he can be thrown down.

72

73

Combined attack is a series of attacking techniques performed continually, without stopping. *It is necessary to practise them very much, to accept the habit of executing punches and kicks in series, and to use them successfully in the ring.* Good combination does not allow the opponent to recover from punches or kicks he received and to counter attack. There are many combinations and everybody should choose those that best suit their temperament and abilities. Some fighters combine punches and knee kicks, others prefer various foot and punch techniques, but this is not of greatest importance. If the combination is good, it will prove itself in a ring. Several combinations described in this chapter will serve as examples to the reader. They were also proved valid in matches as all combinations accepted in Thai Boxing. There are no theoretical combinations in Muay Thai. Very popular and frequent combination is a double round kick (photo 1, 2, 3). The essence of this combination is to provoke the opponent to counter attack or to disturb his concentration with the first kick delivered into his leg. Round kick into his thigh almost unconsciously makes him drop his hands, as he is put off balance. This is the right moment for the delivery of another kick, this time to his neck or head, (ph. 2). Both round kicks should be performed in one continuous motion, and good balance is required. Again, while kicking, hands must protect our head, as we are very vulnerable while standing on one leg only! Even if the opponent does not drop his hands, we can kick him again in the thigh. There are many Thai boxers who perform a series of four or five kicks in just a few seconds. Another very popular combination is a straight punch followed by a round kick (photo 4, 5). Straight punches (jabs) can disturb the opponent in a ring. At the moment his attention loosens a very fast round kick should be delivered. This combination uses another subconscious reaction; that is an opponent's lifting hands in order to protect his head, while his body remains unprotected.

It is necessary to perform this combination very fast in the match. The first kick shakes the opponent, while the following hits him on his head. After lowering the kicking foot of the first kick, it is necessary to spring powerfully for the next.

1

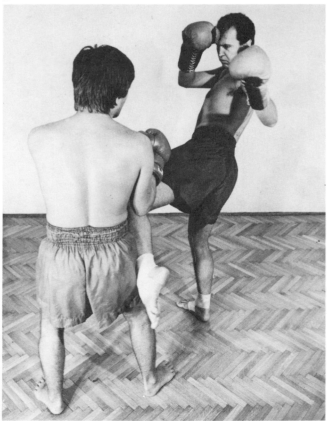

2

3

4

Very common combination: straight punch followed by a round kick with shin. A shin kick is very often used as the finishing technique in Thai Boxing, though in other martial arts it is almost unknown. Before delivering round shin kick, the left foot steps to the side and slightly forward. It is characteristic of Thai Boxing that almost all techniques are performed with a small step which increases power.

5

6

7

Similar combinations can be seen in photos 6-9. This time we attack with two fast straight punches: right first and then with the left reverse punch. As the opponent tries to counter attack we step to the side with the left foot and deliver a round shin kick into his body (ph.9).

10

8

9

Photographs 10 and 11 show another simple combination consisting of two foot techniques. First we disturb opponent's concentration with one or several front kicks. When his attention loosens or when he decides to counter attack, we step to the side with the right foot and deliver a round kick into his body. Arms should be kept in front of the head, as on photo 11.

11

12

13

14

Very effective short combinations are shown in photos 12, 13, 14. First we attack the opponent with front kicks, the same as in a previous combination. When he tries to counter attack, we deliver a left knee kick, at the same time blocking his punch with the double arm cover. Clashing with the knee, the opponent increases the power of the kick himself.

Certain equipment is necessary in order to practice basic techniques, attacks and defences. Elementary equipment for Thai Boxing is: kicking and punching bags and pads, protective equipment (headgear, mouthguard, bandages, cotton anklets and genital protectors), sparring gloves, light leather punching gloves, trunks or training suit and different weights. Photo 1. shows the most necessary equipment.

Though Thai Boxing can be practiced without this equipment, it should be obtained, as it enables us to kick and punch with full power. Kicking and punching with the use of equipment develops feeling of distance and power; therefore progress is faster. Some beginners can start sparring practice after a few months of such training!

Thai boxers usually practice twice a day; early in the morning and in the afternoon or in the evening. Training lasts about two hours. Before starting to practice boxers usually run a few miles, so that they do not need any special warming up exercises. There are no unnecessary ceremonial salutes or bows, as in similar martial arts. When the trainer starts the stop-watch training has started. All the exercises last three minutes and there is one minute rest.

The trainer informs his students of the last half minute of the round, and then they try to practice with maximum power and speed in order to be ready for a match. The first few rounds of the training schedule are devoted to shadow boxing ("dtoi lom"). It is a fight with an imaginary opponent using all the techniques in a boxer's repetoire (photo 2). Boxers practice shadow boxing relaxed but fast. In Thai boxing speed is essential. Slow kicks or punches are only a waste of power. After "dtoi lom" boxers start to practice defence and attack combinations.

1

Photo 1. Equipment of Thai Boxing. On the left side are kicking and punching pads (used for practicing on a moving target). Below are light leather gloves for practice on punching bag. On the top are heavy 16 ounce gloves for sparring. At the bottom are trunks used by Thai Boxers, cup and cotton anklets.

Photo 2. There are no special rules for shadow boxing. Everybody practises his own combinations. During training only a hissing sound can be heard from exhaling air, while executing punches and kicks.

2

Combined attacks can be best learned with the partner who holds kicking and punching pads. Combinations may consist of two, up to five or six connected strikes. A series of techniques is executed on the kicking and punching pads, while the partner who holds them retreats. Kicks and punches should be connected as fast as possible. A series of photos will show the reader how Thai Boxers exercise combinations. The first example shows the combination of two punches and a round kick (ph.3-7).

Two straight punches (left and then right) are made from the basic stance (ph. 3,4). Then sidestepping with the right foot (ph. 5) a left round kick is delivered (ph. 6 and 7). In the rear of the photograph, boxers winding up bandages for punching bag practice, can be seen.

Photograph left: A powerful knee kick as the finishing technique of a very fast combination.

3

4

Thai Boxing training is based on a boxer's individual work. The trainer spends part of the time with every boxer. There are no strict line-ups, no counting as in Japanese Karate for example. But everybody knows that his fighting ability depends on how hard he trains.

5

6

7

8

9

In the following example we can see the combination consisting of straight punch followed by two knee kicks (ph. 8, 9, 10). Left (leading) straight punch is delivered first (ph. 8) and then we step forward with the right foot and deliver a powerful kick with the left knee springing sharply from the floor. Immediately, the right knee kick follows (ph. 9, 10). The next combination is just a foot techniques combination. After executing a front kick (ph.11) we step forward and to the side and deliver a round kick (ph. 13). Combination consists of two kicks executed with the same foot while moving in.

10

11

12

13

Defence combinations are practiced so that the partner attacks with different techniques (round kick for example — photo 14) and we block or evade and then perform several counter attacks, connects into series. The main purpose of practicing defence combinations is to connect blocks and counterattacks as fast as possible.

After about ten rounds of practice on kicking and punching pads, practice with a partner follows (ph.16, 17, 18). One of the partners attacks first, while the other defends using different techniques. In the following round partners exchange roles. In this phase of training, protective equipment is still not used, as kicks and punches are not delivered with full power. The purpose of this part of the training is to improve a fighter's ability of defending while moving in the space. After several rounds of such practice, work on punching and kicking bag follows.

14

15

16

17

18

Photographs show an example of attack and defence exercises with the partner. The Boxer on the left side defends himself against round kicks by blocking with his shin and then counter attacks. Later roles are exchanged.

A very important part of each training session is practice on kicking and punching bags. Bags can vary in size and hardness, but usually punching bags are lighter. In the majority of schools, they use the same bag for punching and kicking. Bag practice increases kicking and punching power, strengthens fists, shins and knees. Some short combinations, especially punching and knee techniques can be exercised too. Even after a month of practice great improvement can be noticed. Kicks, punches and the body as a whole will be more powerful, combinations faster and stamina better. For punching techniques the fist should be bandaged to avoid eventual injuries if punches are not delivered correctly. Light leather gloves should also be worn. Bag practice should last about ten rounds, and if we practice seriously, it is very tiring. During this ten rounds all the basic techniques and combinations should be performed. Here are some combinations on a kicking bag (ph.20, 21, 22). After the front kick with the right foot, it is lowered and a left round kick and right knee follow.

Series of photographs 23-26 show initial posture and two round knee kicks.

While executing the kicks, elbows and forearms should be kept close to the bag. Photographs 27 and 28 show front knee kick with a grab. In training, knee combinations can consist of up to ten knee kicks. It is not uncommon that Thai Boxers spend several rounds practicing only various knee kicks.

19

Photo 19. Top boxers use jumping knee kick ("join kao"). It is one of the most dangerous techniques in Muay Thai.

20

21

22

23

24

Grab ("djab ko") and a series of round kicks with the knee is an essential part of training with the kicking bag. Swinging motion of the body and hip rotation increases power of the kick. Two or three rounds of such practice is a minimum for every serious training.

98

25

26

27

28

Close range fighting with the knee is an art, where nobody is better than Thai boxers. Not without reason. They practice knee techniques very hard. During the match, the tactic of some boxers known as "knee specialists" is to insist on close distance fighting, where they are best in knee techniques. You can recognise such fighters by strong body and leg muscles (ph.27, 28).

Sparrring practice is the most important part of Thai Boxing training schedule. Knowledge attained during training is tested in sparring. Reflexes, movements and different combinations here come to practical usage. Most important, personal style of fighting is developed. No other exercise can replace sparring. During sparring practice boxers wear protective equipment (cup and headgear) in order to avoid unnecessary injuries. It is important that a trainer or experienced friend watch you during sparring so that they can point out your mistakes afterwards. There are several kinds of sparring in Thai Boxing. They depend on techniques that are used: punching techniques, sparring, knee sparring and free sparring. Somebody who has not mastered basic techniques cannot begin with sparring practice. Three or five months of intensive training are usually required. Thais call sparring "len chen".

Photo 29. Muang Surin boxers during sparring.

29

Sparring with only punching techniques

This in fact is identical to western boxing, but bending too much forward is avoided as in a real fight it increases the risk of receiving a knee kick. Sixteen ounce gloves are worn (ph.30, 31). Muang Surin boxers are well known for their superb hand techniques among Muay Thai fighters. Through this kind of sparring boxers learn how to dodge, move and attack in different directions and how to connect punches into series. Thai Boxing differs from karate and Kung fu in its dynamics and changes of the directions of the attack and defence. It seems that Karate and many Kung fu styles prefer direct clashes with one decisive blow.

30

31

This improves a boxer's close fighting abilities. Only knee kicks with grabs and throws are allowed. This is the most exhausting way of sparring, as many wrestling techniques are mixed with knee kicks. Genital protectors should be worn under the trunks, because during exchanging knee kicks one can be easily hurt. It is very important to learn to use the opponent's power against him and to direct him in the way we want. Releasing and escaping from dangerous situations is also learned during this kind of sparring. Every Thai boxer has a solid repertoire of such techniques, and great stamina is achieved by regular practice. (ph. 32).

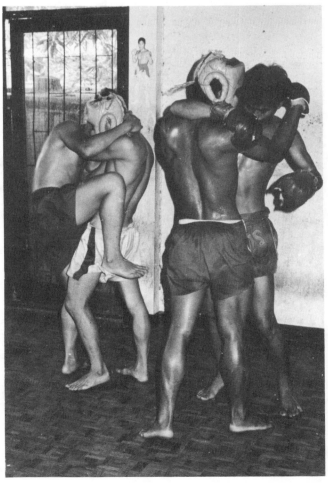

32

All techniques except elbow strikes are used in free sparring (ph. 33). The purpose of this exercise is to learn to fight together with the partner, not to prove one's superiority. Therefore mutual confidence and reliability should be established with a partner to avoid elements that hinder progress. Mistakes and blows received during sparring should be accepted in an attitude of sportsmanship. It is necessary to be relaxed during sparring, so that we can react with maximum speed. All previously learned combinations and counters should be applied in sparring. It usually lasts five rounds, though boxers often spar fifteen rounds before some important matches. Patience is very important, too. Unless we are certain that we can hit the target we should not attack. All sorts of tricks should be used. Fakes should look convincing so that, making the opponent believe in our intentions, we create openings. Here are some examples: after feinting straight punch into the head, we deliver low round kick or vice versa. There is also many "low-up" and "left-right" feinting; for example we fake low round kick and execute high section round kick, or we fake left uppercut and execute right hook, etc. False attacks can be made too, in order to cheat the opponent. In this case the first technique is false and the second hits the opponent. Though false attacks are usually executed with less power, we must take care that they look believable. An example: we attack the opponent with the low round kick, he blocks with his shin, and then immediately we deliver the next kick into his supporting leg. This of course, must be made before he starts his own counter-attack. It is also important to strive to break the opponent's rhythm by, for example, retreating and then suddenly counter attacking. There is great field for research and the number of possibilities is almost infinite. Everybody must explore and experiment persistently on his own. Besides progress in techniques of fighting, sparring develops confidence which is very important in a match. After sparring, a trainer's advice must be listened to carefully, and we must try not to do the same mistakes again.

At the end of the training, strength exercises should be practised. They are similar to those in other martial arts and will not be described in this book in detail. Usual exercises are push ups, legs ups, sit ups, weight lifting, etc. There is a special kind of small weight that can be held by the fists, and can be used for shadow boxing. Though these exercises are the least interesting and practiced at the end of the training when everybody is tired, they should not be neglected, as strength and endurance are very important in matches.

A technically good, but physically not well prepared fighter, will lose his power in the first rounds of a match and will be easily defeated. Badly prepared fighters suffer most injuries, too. As Thai boxers are usually well prepared, serious injuries are, unexpectedly, very rare.

33

Martial arts literature very often describes the so called "inner power", ("Chi" in Chinese or "Ki" in Japanese). Many books mention certain old masters who possessed high control of "Chi" and their unbelievable ability; for example to break ten bricks just by pressing them with palm ("iron palm technique"), or to kill an opponent by only touching him ("death touch")!

Some instructors claim that they possess "Chi", but their demonstrations are only tricks and frauds or fakirism. The author of this book saw such demonstrations a few times, unfortunately from some very well known instructors who teach in Europe and USA. *One thing is certain, no book can give the practitioner inner strength. You must find it on your own.* It can only be attained through years of hard training and is manifested not like some mysterious power, but through ability to sustain hardships, critical moments, in concentrated reactions with all mind and body potentials, and never giving up.

The Marble Temple (Wat Benchamabopitr).

One evening, in front of Rachadamneon stadium in Bangkok, trainer Dentharonee Muangsurin introduced me to meet several friends, former fighters and trainers from different schools of Thai Boxing. While we were drinking juice in a small reataurant near the stadium, we had a very interesting conversation. Later, according to my memory, I wrote down some fragments in the form of advice for fighting. Please read them carefully, because they originate from years of hard training and experience from hundreds of matches.

1. *Always look straight at the opponent.*
2. *Keep your mouth shut (in order to protect teeth and tongue).*
3. *Be always relaxed except when delivering kick or punch.*
4. *Never turn your back to the opponent.*
5. *Never try the technique that you have not completely mastered.*
6. *Never concentrate on an attack or defence, only.*
7. *When you attack, take care of your safety.*
8. *If the opponent is taller, impose a close range fight, if he is shorter, impose fight from a distance.*
9. *Never show your emotions: pain, fear, anger, etc.*
10. *Never show exhaustion or signs of fatigue.*
11. *Find out the opponent's weak points by trying different techniques.*
12. *Weaker kick or punch that hits the target is better than powerful one that missed.*
13. *Faster blows should be used from distance, while stronger from close range.*
14. *Never miss the chance for a successful attack. The chance you missed might not appear again.*
15. *Don't waste your power. You will need it at the end of the match.*
16. *Never underestimate the opponent. Never have the feeling of superiority, but also keep in mind that anybody, regardless of reputation, can lose.*
17. *Even defeat is a part of a victory for a good fighter, as it will help him to realize his mistakes.*

Left: Promoter Sa Non and Thai bantam category champion Samaransak Muangsurin, on a press conference prior to Samaransak's title defending match.
Bottom: Group photograph before training.

Thai Boxing was almost unknown throughout the world until a few years ago. The reasons were influx of Hong Kong's martial arts films and masses of instructors from far east, who appeared in USA and Europe offering high ranks, without much sweat, but for a lot of money. Various Kung fu schools and Karate styles grew like mushrooms after rain. There are hundreds of Bruce Lee "students", and there are many styles which one could not find in their homeland: Japan, Korea or China. In spite of this, Thai Boxing was slowly entering the world. It was first introduced to Japan in 1964. There, under the name of "Kickboxing" with the help of live TV transmissions, it soon became more popular than Karate. Matches between Japanese kickboxers and Thais were very attractive. In the beginning the Japanese had to learn a lot from Thai boxers but soon they mastered the Thai game. On August 20, 1972, Japanese kickboxer Mitsuo Shima from Meyiro school defeated a Thai champion by winning on points. He was the first foreigner to defeat a Thai champion, and in Bangkok at that. In the following years many Japanese kickboxers won the titles, to mention just the most popular as: Okao, Yamasato brothers, Shiba, Fujiwara and others. In USA Kickboxing was introduced during the seventies and quickly became serious rivals of "Full Contact" whose father is Jhoon Rhee, Korean Taekwondo master. An American Raymond Edler spent some time living in Bangkok and was the only non-Thai fighter to enter the top ten list of Rachadamneon stadium. He was the fifth in middle weight category and later competed in Japan where he became champion.

Dave Kwalheim, a US service man trained in Chiang Mai, a town in the north of Thailand where he defeated some of the best boxers in the province. Benny Urquides from Mexico, a USA Full contact champion, had some success in matches with Japanese kickboxers, though he fought with somewhat modified rules. His match with Narongnoi Grianbundit, one of the top Thai fighters ended in a draw. In September, 1983, in Bangkok at Rachadamneon stadium, one of the top American Full contact fighters, Don Wilson tried his luck against Thai champion Samaad Prasamit from Konken province. Don Wilson was nine kilos heavier, and during five round match was knocked down twice. He was defeated on points and after the match declared to news reporters that he would start learning Thai Boxing. After the USA, Muay Thai entered Europe. There are clubs in Holland, England, France and Germany. The best known are Meyiro and Chakuriki in Holland and Yamatsuki in France. Some Europeans had matches

in Thailand. During my stay in Thailand I saw a match between Ronny Green from England and a well known Bangkok fighter Sirimongkol Trachohae. Ronny won in the second round by k.o.!

He learnt Muay Thai in Udon Thani a small town in the North of Thailand, where he spent more than a year.

On April 17, 1983 in Jaap Edenhal in Holland one of the biggest Thai Boxing events took place. There were 5000 spectators watching the best European kickboxers fighting some Thai boxers. Though boxers from Thailand were not champions (as it was announced), matches proved that Europeans still have to learn a lot. But the public was so enthusiastic and Thai Boxing is attaining its public following. Some matches ended with an ovation. It is a pity that real Thai Champions have not yet come to Europe, and it will take a long time before Europeans reach their level.

Thais are right to be proud of their martial art.

top: author during training in Muang-Surin school.
right: with the trainer Dentharonee Muangsurin.

left: trainer Surapong Harmnyom and author.

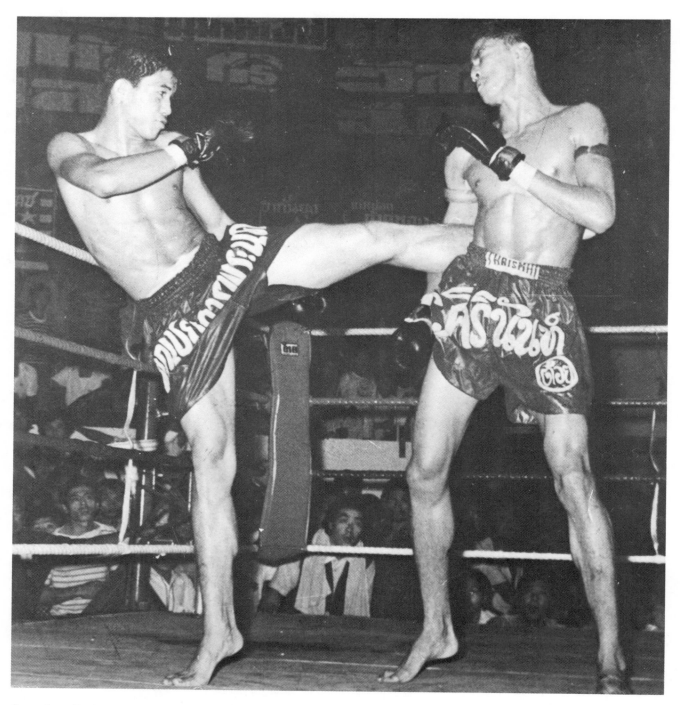

Scene from Rachadamneon stadium.

A LINE FROM AN OLD MANUSCRIPT ON THAI BOXING:

Top boxers are as rare as diamonds. Their edges are cut by years of training,
their techniques are polished to perfection as the surface of the glittering diamond; magnificent
in its beauty and unique in its strength.

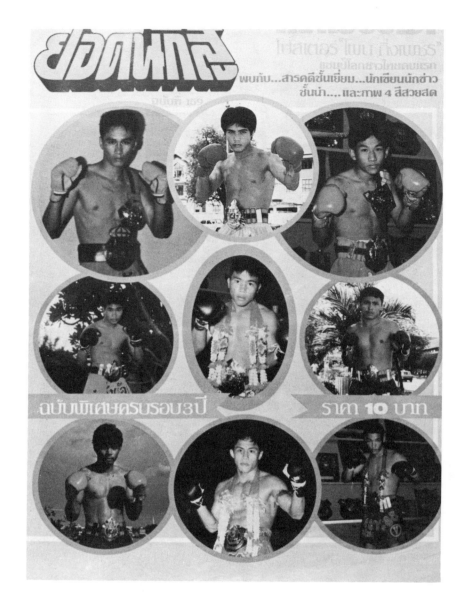

Thai boxing champions in season 1982/83:
Dissennoi Sovorokunchai, Samara Payacalun, Chamua Pet
Hapalan, Pallannoi Kietalan, Paraha Lek Sitchunton, Rang-
sak Pontovi, Sensaxda Kitigasen, Kontorony Payacalun,
Jamhod Luksamlon.

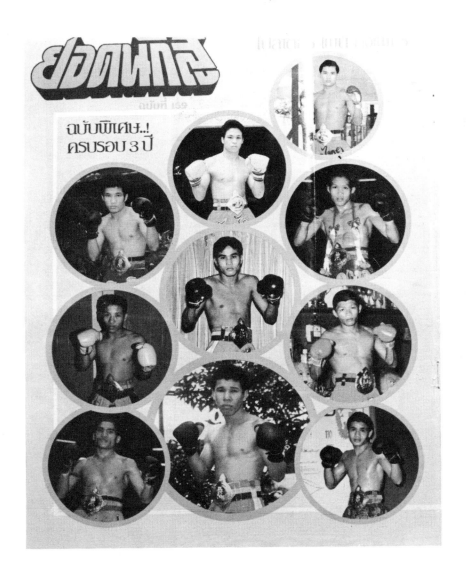

Kity Soatanicum, Rakchai Nipovithandy, Kumpolnnoi Taetai, Lenelong Tailunleon, Insinnoi Soatinicum, Legsaknnoi Lousungkam, Lankun Kitlecai, Kautsot Sitpapom, Payannoi Soatatseny, Nompon Chumpuntong.

And finally, to all those who became interested and have started practicing Thai Boxing with the help of this book I would recommend to make a diary of their training. Lengths of parts of their training (warming up, bag and pads practice, sparring, strength exercises) should be noted here. Also, techniques that were not performed well during training should be noted and analysed later. They should be corrected in the following training sessions. After some time if you train regularly and seriously you will notice progress.

This table may serve as an example of the training diary.

	sun.	mon.	tue.	wed.	thur.	fri.	sat.
warming up							
rope skipping							
running							
shadow boxing							
punching and							
kicking pads practice							
bag practice							
power exercise							
notice							

I wish you successful training.